DARK PSYCH

The secret techniques to analyze and interpret people, improve your persuasion and avoid deception and manipulation.

Robert Dawn

INTRODUCTION

"Let's not forget that the causes

of human actions are usually

immeasurably more complex

and varied than our explanations

subsequent ones on them."

Fyodor Dostoyevsky

Psychology in general is concerned with the study and understanding of human behavior: thoughts, emotions, actions and interactions with other people. In particular, dark psychology focuses on thoughts, emotions, actions and interactions that are predatory in nature. It focuses on the tactics used to manipulate, persuade, motivate in the desired direction and coerce others so that their actions benefit the manipulator. Dark psychology, therefore, can be analyzed as the study of the characteristics of the human condition in order to take advantage of it. This psychology aims to understand these thoughts, feelings, perceptions and interactions, so that it can then be applied to take advantage of others. Whether it is applied to achieve a certain behavior in another person or to know how much influence one has over others. It is usually applied for specific reasons, although in some cases it is applied to brutally victimize for no rational purpose.

In religions these techniques are usually applied in a subtle way in some cases and in others, where religion is transformed into fanaticism, they are applied in a forceful way without leaving any room for doubt.

Religion blames the devil or a negative entity for the evil within humanity, it does not directly blame the human being, but considers him a victim of this negative entity.

It can be said that all human beings have a dark side, in some it is a slight aspect, in others a little more marked and in others it is not noticeable because the person is in charge of hiding it very well and brings it out when he needs to use it. These people present themselves as the lambs that hide the real wolf.

The personality traits that give rise to the dark side of human beings are: narcissism, Machiavellianism, psychopathy and sadism. These characteristics are the ones that originate the mistreatment of others.

Advertising also applies dark psychology seeking to increase sales, generating need in the people who see the ads. In addition, they consider them as dehumanized prospects to be convinced that they need this or that product to live better or overcome their problems. The drug industry also applies these same principles, trying to get people to resort to them every time they feel an ailment.

These people act knowing that they are seeking to manipulate for profit and, in most cases, have no scruples or conscience and are not even interested in thinking about the consequences they are generating with their actions or communications.

The most extreme manifestations of dark psychology are necrophiliacs, serial killers, torturers, rapists, psychopaths and sociopaths. People who only find satisfaction in the brutal deeds they are capable of carrying out.

In this book we will not analyze the extreme cases of dark psychology, but will focus on the analysis of cases that people are confronted with almost daily in their everyday lives.

CHAPTER 1
WHAT DOES IT MEAN TO MANIPULATE

"Knowing your own darkness

is the best method to deal with the

darkness from other people."

Carl Gustav Jung

A simple and straightforward definition of manipulation is perhaps: "To manipulate is to handle at will something or someone". If it is about objects, using manipulation is acceptable since I can take it, use it and then discard it or keep it depending on whether I can use it again in the future or not. But if it is about people, it is understood that the interactions or the way of relating to each other, is of equal conditions, in which the capacities and possibilities of the initiative are respected. If a person relates to others thinking that they are susceptible to be handled at will, he/she is lowering people to the level of objects. This mode of relating is called sadism, of varying degrees, but ultimately the relationship becomes sadistic. It would seem that people act with cruelty on others and in a certain way it is, although the one who exercises it is not always conscious of his cruelty. In some cases the person is aware of it. But in all cases there is a great underestimation of the other person and his intellectual capacity, since he considers that he will not realize it.

This type of interaction can also be seen in couple relationships. When a man seeks to have a beautiful woman by his side to exhibit her as a trophy, he is not looking at the person, but rather he is looking for an object that at the same time turns out to be a trophy and gives him a certain status within his social group. Even in intimacy this object relationship can be seen as the only thing that is present is physical beauty and how much this excites him. The person, in cases like this, is blurred, her values, her tastes, her ideas, nothing is important in front of the fact that she is a very beautiful woman.

Another example of manipulation is the trafficking of people, who are taken from one place to another, with the purpose of being exploited in a certain job. This work can be either in an industry or in sexual exploitation. These people are treated as slaves, they are convinced that from now on this will be the life they will lead, without any rights.

On the other hand, in ancient times, marriages were arranged and, logically, the woman was very young and had no say. They were an object of negotiation, as was their dowry. They were placed below the rank of a person, violating their most elementary rights.

In the workplace, when a new person enters the company, it is common to consider him/her as a potential enemy who comes to take away what we rightfully believe to be ours. Although with the passage of time it is demonstrated that they did not come to take anything, the initial bad moments they made them go through. Some call it "paying the right to the floor".

Another way of considering manipulation is the way of socially influencing in order to modify behaviors and perceptions about certain things or people, using indirect and deceitful strategies. The person who exercises manipulation in this way advances socially at the expense of others.

Sometimes manipulation is used with the intention of benefiting the other person, although the other person is not able to see it that way. The most common example in this sense is the action that parents often take on their children so that they make the right decisions, such as eating healthy or studying. This is also a form of manipulation.

This type of influence may be harmless and irrelevant as far as social intercourse is concerned. There is no coercion or malice, although there is a clear intent to do one's own bidding over what the children want or desire. Perhaps the parents are right to do so or not, regardless of that, they are exercising manipulation over their children. If the children are young,

do not have a choice unless the parents offer it to them. If the children are of an older age, they will certainly be able to oppose the parents' requests, even if the parents try to manipulate them.

The manipulative person does not let his intentions be seen and if he is directly rebuked, he assumes the position of victim. They usually start their actions in a casual way, seeking to please while analyzing the other person's reactions. Little by little, the manipulator envelops the other person with flattery and words of empathy, until he/she finally gets him/her to lower his/her guard and open up, attacking at that moment with all his/her potential.

In all these manipulations, we will see that some are more harmful than others. If it is an advertisement that urges healthy eating and sports, it could be considered a harmless manipulation. If it is about people seeking to have a certain body, then this influence can be harmful or very harmful depending on the reaction of the person who looks at it. There are people who get sick for not achieving the ideals of beauty or spend all their salary to achieve a wardrobe that brings them closer to that ideal, developing a real obsession with this issue.

When getting to know a person, it is necessary to analyze what kind of behavior he/she has with others: if he/she is a person who exercises natural leadership or some kind of influence, it is essential to be attentive to him/her, because at some point he/she will try to manipulate us. Believing that "she won't manipulate me" is opening the door to manipulation. Sometimes the more harmless a person appears to be, the more dangerous he or she can become.

CHAPTER 2
TRAITS OF A PERSON HANDLER

"Take your distance from people.

that never admit to being wrong,

and they consider it all your fault."

Anonymous

When you understand how simple it can be to be a manipulator, you can see the true scope of emotional manipulation. The strategies used in manipulation are a derivation of existing methods of control. Generally, there is no awareness of this manipulation, which leads one to believe that the manipulator applies the strategies intelligently because the victim does not notice. The most dangerous manipulators are those who do detailed and cold planning without considering the implications for the victim. Manipulators are cold, aggressive, opportunistic, insensitive people who only think of their own benefit. They usually have serious psychological disorders, although sometimes they are people with a normal psychology who seek their own benefit.

Two basic types of manipulation can be evaluated: eventual manipulators and compulsive manipulators with pathological behavior. These compulsive manipulators know no other way of relating to the world than through manipulation.

The eventual manipulators do know how to relate differently with the rest of the world and choose with whom they will manipulate.

Emotional manipulation is achieving a significant wear and tear on the person, undermining their self-confidence and altering their perceptions of the world. This degradation is gradual and occurs without the victim noticing it. In general, the victim trusts the perpetrator and therein lies the key to the control he exercises. In some cases, the faith that this person has in the manipulator is a blind faith and allows him to make all the decisions.

The manipulator only thinks about winning, no matter if he succeeds in convincing as long as he achieves his goal. When one accepts what the manipulator says without understanding the reasons why this or that behavior is requested, one adheres to a gregarious behavior whose actions are determined by the person who leads. In this way, minds and wills are molded to the whim of a single person.

A clear example of this is the religious leaders who lead their followers not to accept traditional medicine or not to allow a transfusion even when their life depends on it or the life of a loved one. What the leader told them is followed without question, considering that traditional medicine will only harm them.

In the case of salespeople, there are some who speak in favor of a product with the sole intention of selling it. They do not take into account the buyer's needs, but only try to convince him by putting into play the strategies they know. In addition, they limit their offer to a number of products and set a time frame, generating a feeling of scarcity and that the opportunity is now or never.

In other cases, they mark a level of status with that product, so that, by acquiring it, they become a select group of the society in which they live. This is very common in the automotive industry. For example: advertising where a man drives with a beautiful lady sitting next to him, driving through dreamy places, with a background music that invites to romance and a very quiet voice that says *"Enjoy the deepest emotions"*.

At no point in the advertisement is the fact of buying the car mentioned, but rather it speaks of the experiences that will be obtained only by driving the car. They mark masculine power, seduce with an image, stimulate desire and, of course, override the will to think. The price is not mentioned, only the senses, passions and desires are fed.

All this without forgetting that it resorts to the most common social stereotypes: the man with power who controls everything and the woman as a decorative figurine or trophy to arouse admiration or envy and generating a certificate of successful man.

If when you go shopping, you direct your attention to the most advertised products, you must understand that the manipulation is having an effect on your psyche. The purchase decision you make will surely be based on the advertisements you saw and, even if you have not paid much attention to them, they are still incorporated in your mind, in your unconscious.

In general, this is the most common type of manipulation that can be found in the different orders of life. It is usually called demagogy instead of manipulation. Demagogy is a form of tyranny based on flattery and false promises, a double discourse that marks one type of action even when the demagogue performs a very different one. The word demagogy usually has political connotations and history shows that, if a way of thinking is adopted and maintained as an unalterable program, it becomes charged with emotionality even when it ceases to be a persuasive discourse.

Unlike the manipulative person, the one who spreads his ideas frankly and explains his reasons, allowing others to listen and give their opinion, is not manipulating, and even when his ideas are wrong, at no time does he try to deceive or convince. He allows others to choose for themselves.

Some parents believe that guiding their children in the family values they received is manipulation. In reality, everything that means family values are experienced and learned gradually, it is very rare that they are taught in a coercive way.

The person who wants to manipulate spends his time studying the psychology of the masses, how they work, how they act in his favor. In general, he is an attractive and charismatic person who is well liked because his first actions seem disinterested. But it is only a start, then he will act to obtain your benefit.

For example: automation is a good strategy to achieve profitability, but it transforms an operator, who is also a person with his own characteristics, into a piece of a gear from which he cannot get out and which does not allow him to develop to his full potential. It is necessary that these automated and repetitive processes are carried out by a machine instead of a person.

Manipulators do not point to the fundamental aspects of the issue, but focus on secondary details with the intention of diverting attention by impressing their listeners. He never offers a global picture or an approach from different perspectives, he uses clichés that are socially accepted as a way into the minds of his listeners.

He is not interested in seeking the truth but in imposing himself and defeating his opponent by using language that may be ambiguous or give rise to different interpretations.

For example: when a real estate agency wants to sell a small house, it does not say "it is a small house" but it says "it is a cozy house that seeks family togetherness". It is a half-truth that seeks to generate emotions.

The manipulative person, on the other hand, does not encourage dialogue as a way of clarifying different points or ideas. They do not seek space for an exchange of points of view, but rather seek acceptance of their perspective at all times through a well-crafted discourse.

It also makes use of current trends to achieve greater effectiveness, for example:

Freedom is not having to face any obstacles.

The average person is looking for quick and easy, recipe-type solutions.

The average person needs to avoid conflict to maintain peace because it is what makes them feel safe.

Manipulators can easily recognize those people who have a greater predisposition to be manipulated because they are insecure with a tendency to emotional fragility, they are sensitive and empathic people, who are often afraid of loneliness and very concerned about the opinion of others with fear of being a disappointment. In addition, they tend to be very emotionally dependent.

An insecure person is easily identified because of the tendency to be defensive at the slightest attack or when under pressure. The manipulator does not need a great deal of interaction to detect her, but he will make his inroads to detect her in her entirety. Based on that, the handler will have her in his sights for when he needs her.

Some people will demonstrate social anxiety, which will lead to the conclusion that he/she is a person with emotional fragility, which will be exposed because he/she breaks down easily. This condition of fragility is temporary so the manipulator should seize the moment.

As for people who are sensitive, they understand life at a deep level with the ability to grasp the details and subtleties of social relationships. They avoid hurting others and dislike all manifestations of violence. Manipulators manifest to have emotional burdens that they seek to pass on to this type of person and from there they begin their manipulation. The person who manipulates will approach because he/she knows that by education he/she will not be rejected and will try to please him/her.

Other people who are subject to frequent manipulation are empaths. They are sensitive people who have a great capacity to tune in to the feelings of others. In order to manipulate them, you are likely to fake emotions that you do not feel and are very likely to swindle them commercially or financially.

Another group of people vulnerable to the attacks of this type of predator are people who are afraid of loneliness. For this reason, they are capable of accepting any type of company that avoids loneliness, including a relationship of submission or abuse. Manipulators approach them as friends or ideal partners and when they gain their trust they begin the process of swindling. People abandoned in childhood are the ones who feel the most loneliness and the ones who fall more frequently.

People who are afraid of disappointing other people and who are capable of anything to avoid disappointment are also victims. We all suffer from this type of fear, but in some people it becomes pathological and dangerous. Sometimes this type of fear influences family relationships and the person does everything he/she can to avoid disappointing those closest to him/her. Other times, this fear extends to all the people he/she knows.

Finally, manipulators are also victims of manipulators, those people who relate to others through a relationship of emotional dependence. In general, they are people who are afraid of losing their affections and therefore become submissive, obedient and extremely careful. In every decision they are going to make, they have to consult their loved ones and they need them to agree with what they are going to do. All the time they need the advice and opinion of people who are significant to them. This is what manipulators use against them. They approach them, solve their problems, support them unconditionally and this comfort they generate in the dependent person is their most common strategy.

CHAPTER 3
WHAT DOES IT MEAN TO PERSUADE

"The art of persuasion consists of

both in terms of pleasing and convincing;

since men are governed more by

by whim than by reason."

Blaise Pascal

In these times, persuasion is installed in every aspect of the human being: in advertisements, in the workplace, in human interactions, in political and religious discourses, and in interactions with loved ones.

Persuasion is the ability to communicate in such a way as to convince the viewer to think this or that way, modify his or her beliefs or behavior.

Persuasion has tools and strategies that aim to bring out emotions and from there, modify their thoughts, it is not mind control but it does have the tendency to control the minds of others. This modality of control has been studied since ancient times by the first Greek philosophers. They were great orators and knew how to use words to make themselves understood and to convince. In general, great orators are highly persuasive people.

Aristotle, in his studies, divided persuasion into 3 parts: *ethos, logos and pathos*. He called *ethos* the credibility of the speaker. Aristotle could see that, if the speaker addressed his audience with confidence and conviction, he appeared in the eyes of his audience as an expert on the subject. His message was received much more favorably than that of speakers who showed nervousness or hesitation or even stammered.

The second part, called *logos* meaning logic, was taken into account because he discovered that the speech had to contain logical aspects that would form its basis. Aristotle considered that reasoning makes the audience suppose that an important conclusion has been reached by their own deduction, when in fact they were skillfully led by the speaker.

The *pathos* part is the emotional strategy that leads to achieving the result sought. That is to say, the mood predisposition that is achieved through the words that were said and that lead to the conclusion. This is the main point of persuasion currently in use, i.e., targeting the emotional aspects of the subject in order to raise awareness.

For example: commercials with their slogans, colors, jingles, beautiful people who are happy and dreaming of wonderful worlds, etc. Suddenly a person is watching his or her favorite program and the commercials come on. It is almost certain that the person does not pay attention to them consciously, but unconsciously, it sticks in his mind and it is almost certain that at some point he will buy one of the advertised products. It is like when you see an advertisement for potato chips and you feel like eating them. It is a contagious effect.

All these kinds of things are deeply studied by market researchers and how persuasion is involved in the whole process. It is also widely studied how persuasion acts on the human mind and how it translates into everyday actions.

In a normal conversation, the person presenting an idea uses words to do so consciously, achieving an emotional response in the other person. Generally speaking, the hope is to achieve the empathy of the other person, which is why, to a greater or lesser extent, everyone tries to be persuasive when communicating with others. The level of success will be greater or lesser, depending on the oratory of each person. The people who have the highest level of persuasion are those who are aware of their own thoughts and reactions, so they know how persuasion works from their own experience.

CHAPTER 4

PRINCIPLES OF PERSUASION BY ROBERT CIALDINI

"Civilization is victory

of persuasion over force."

Plato

To gain an understanding of persuasion techniques and how they are currently used in society, it is necessary to analyze the studies carried out by Dr. Richard Cialdini, set forth in his book *The Psychology of Persuasion* published in 1984. As Professor Emeritus of Psychology and Marketing at Arizona State University, he explained his principles in a simple way that is continually applied in product marketing.

Among the famous people who have used its principles is Donald Trump, who based his political campaign on them. These principles clarify each of the aspects into which psychological persuasion can be broken down and he presents them as follows:

Principle of reciprocity: it is the action that exerts the persuasion since it offers something in exchange for what is asked of it.

Commitment and loyalty: it is the action by which the persuaded person commits to what he/she is going to do and remains with his/her idea once the decision has been made.

Social proof: it is the influence that one has at social level achieving the behavior in masses or gregarious behavior.

Principle of taste: works the persuasion from the side of the taste that the person has and that the persuader exercises.

Principle of authority: the person persuades from his or her position of power and by the mere fact that he or she says so.

Principle of scarcity: just knowing that the product is scarce makes people pay attention to it and buy it.

Need for affiliation: having the need to belong to a group with certain characteristics.

Principle of reciprocity: this principle arises from the social nature of human beings. When a person receives a favor, he or she may feel the need to return the favor or repay it in some way.

For example: the Hare Krishna go around giving a flower or a book and upon acceptance ask for a free-will donation. In this way, they have been able to raise a lot of money. Most people who do a favor do not want a return, but are satisfied with a simple *"thank you"*. This altruistic type of attitude can be taken as a sign of weakness or as diminishing the importance of the favor. One way to assert oneself is to respond *"I know you would do the same for me"*. This type of response generates a sense of indebtedness.

Reciprocity was defined by Cialdini as the action performed by the persuader when he offers a benefit to the person he is trying to persuade in exchange for accepting what he is offering. This benefit may or may not be something that the persuaded person needs, but it will be considered as an opportunity that if he does not accept he will regret. The victim feels indebted to the persuader, because the way he presented it generated in the listener this feeling of being indebted, besides distorting reality in such a way that he appears before his eyes as a disinterested person.

This principle has given very good results in advertising. For example: a product is associated with the image of a famous person, then the person buys it in the belief that in this way he/she will be closer to this famous person with whom he/she has sympathy or likes.

These advertising games are very effective, as if unconsciously providing some kind of security to enter them, even though they are aware that it is only advertising.

Pavlov demonstrated "conditioned reflexes" through dogs that were fed while listening to a bell. After this training, the dogs heard the bell and began to salivate because they knew that food was coming. Humans also have these conditioned reflexes and are able to make these types of unconscious associations. For example: a beer brand associated its name with pleasurable activities such as sailing, skiing, cuddling with a partner, and with this fact managed to increase its sales notoriously.

Another example is a study in which 30 thirsty people were repeatedly shown images of happy people before being made to drink a new soft drink. This led them to consume the product in large quantities and, in addition, to pay for it at three times the value of any other soft drink.

These conditioned reflexes can also be used in a positive way to help people to follow a diet or to motivate them to engage in physical activity. For example: every day at 8 o'clock in the morning I am ready to move my body and enjoy toning it.

Principle of commitment and loyalty: Loyalty is a principle that avoids turning one's back on the group, principle or relationship towards which one has this feeling. Loyalty is closely linked to the conscience of the person and the tacit commitment that this person makes to this group, principle or relationship.

People who value commitment and loyalty are people with a high sense of duty and responsibility. Loyalty and commitment are two values that work together. Loyalty indicates trustworthiness and commitment indicates conviction and consistency with one's beliefs. A committed person is one who fulfills his obligations in excess, that is, a little more than what is expected of him. In the workplace, committed people feel ownership of the company's objectives. When they give their word, they carry this commitment through to the end. Their integrity is fundamental and consistency is the basis for generating trust in others. This is why predators find it possible to manipulate them in this type of loyal and committed people.

Social proof principle: this principle is very powerful because it is based on social consensus. To understand it let's look at the following example: there are two bars, one in front of the other, in one there are so many customers that there are people waiting outside to be served and the other one is empty. When people arrive and see this, 9 out of 10 will wait outside the one that is full and the reason is "as it is full it must be good", "if it is full it must have the best quality or the best prices". This type of behavior is called social proof. That is why marketing often uses slogans that say "we are 200,000 and growing, join this big family". They also use testimonials from people who were satisfied with the product or service.

It has been proven that the products that are best positioned are those that have social consensus. In addition, it has been well studied that advertising should appear on television at times when people are at home resting in front of the TV.

This principle is also used in military training where if soldiers are rested, even if they are given the order to fire on hospitals or innocent civilians, they are not likely to want to do so. But if they are kept 36 hours without sleep, they will be willing to fire on anything without questioning the order. It also applies in police interrogations where a person is kept waiting for so long that an innocent person can be made to plead guilty.

Principle of taste: This principle is based on the fact that people make choices based on what they like. For example, it has been proven that door-to-door salespeople are successful based on their ability to establish a relationship of trust with customers and, as a result, influence them to make purchases. This principle was investigated by Nobel Prize-winning psychologist Daniel Kahneman and Vernon Smith, who laid the foundations of neuroeconomics. They demonstrated that people not only buy from those they like, but that they are able to pay higher prices.

In a few cases these principles are not fulfilled, demonstrating the irrationality of people's thinking. In addition, sometimes these principles are not fulfilled because the person understands that he is under their influence. Sometimes they are not fulfilled due to external influences such as the weather, for example: on cloudy days people tend to feel melancholy so they will not feel willing to buy. On other occasions, meaningless phrases are used with the intention of capturing the listener's attention. For example: the phrase "let me ask you a question for your information", is a phrase that will attract attention because the speaker is saying that the listener will receive information, even though the phrase itself is meaningless. Using this principle, Hollywood studios place commercials within their movies in such a way that they are very natural and even necessary, generating liking for them among people who saw the movie and liked it. The advertising values they manage when they are made in this way are very high because they know that the return they get far exceeds the investment. In the TV series Seinfeld, the main character would say out loud the name of the product and a study showed that when this happened, product sales rates rose. People recognize the influence of advertising on their judgments, but they still allow themselves to be convinced because it is what is socially accepted.

Principle of authority: this principle is evidenced by the fact that people like to obey what an authority says without question. So much so that they may obey even when what they are asked to do is unethical or questionable. An example of this was an experiment conducted at the doors of a bank. The teller was given a sign that read "teller off duty, hand over deposits to the policeman". This policeman was a disguised reporter who had stood next to the teller. Within 2 hours, he was handed about $10,000 in cash and checks, plus social security, credit cards, account numbers, login codes, PINs and many other things that banks say customers don't have to divulge. Only one person hesitated and did not hand anything over to the police. When the rest of the people were asked why they had done so, they replied that he was a policeman. No one had the idea that the policeman might be a fake.

In another experiment, a marketing course was offered in two modalities: the first was given by a well-dressed, refined, athletic man, and the second by an obese, disheveled, poorly dressed man. Out of 10 people, 9 chose the first option because it fulfilled the stereotype of a successful executive. The second was seen as a con man.

It has been proven that, if you enter a place where there is a guard at the entrance who asks *"where are you going?"*, if you enter with a body language that denotes security, determination and authority, the guard will hesitate and will almost certainly not ask because that security will make him think that he is a high official and that asking may be offensive.

Principle of scarcity: this is the tendency to believe that a certain product has limited availability. Either in quantity or in availability over time.

This principle is based on the idea that what is scarce is more valuable than what is plentiful. Auction companies use this principle all the time, especially when several people are bidding for a product. It is also widely used by financial scammers, who tell you not to miss this opportunity or that this is the decision that will change your life. The way to avoid falling for this principle is to be aware of its existence and that a product or service is not going to change anyone's life. There is always something to replace it with.

Need for affiliation: this principle is based on the fact that human beings are sociable and want to live together with other human beings and be accepted and loved in the group they have chosen. Their emotional development plays a very important role as well as their need to depend on the people around them. The need for affiliation is defined as those actions that arise from the search for well-being within the group of belonging.

Most human beings cannot stand being rejected by their close environment and will try to avoid it at all costs. They are likely to go to great lengths to gain the approval of these people. This need for affiliation is completed by the principle of reciprocity and liking. The persuader will use this need to achieve his goal. Their discourse will be oriented to indicate that, if they do such and such a thing, they will obtain the admiration of their group of belonging.

Human beings need to elaborate, show and reinforce the vision they have of themselves and their place in the world, seeking their own affirmation in others.

CHAPTER 5
WAYS TO MANIPULATE

"To effectively manipulate people,

it is necessary to make everyone believe

that no one manipulates them."

John Kenneth Galbraith

One of the ways to carry out a good manipulation is through the gaze. The influence of the gaze is so important that very few people are able to escape it. Some looks attract so naturally that they manage to be looked at without blinking for a prolonged period of time. This gaze reinforces what is being conveyed in oral form and has the ability to suggest. This is also seen in animals as some immobilize their prey through a very intense stare. This stare can be challenging and sometimes annoying to such an extent that the other person ends up averting their gaze. If this happens, you are not achieving what you are looking for with your gaze.

The fascination of the gaze can begin with an unimportant topic and subtle glances, so as to gradually capture the listener's attention and gain his or her gaze as he or she gains a little confidence in what is being said. Without haste, providing space for the other person to express him/herself, a climate will be created where the gaze will be able to have its effect. These steps are necessary for the gaze to have the effect you are looking for, rushing or doing it in a direct way leads the listener to become defensive.

The influence of the gaze is powerful and, when used well, it is a great ally when speaking to an audience. That is why it should not be taken lightly, because it is a real weapon that can be used for defense and, at the same time, as a good offensive. That is why, in order to use it, one must have a strong, focused mind, be able to concentrate and have a deep knowledge of human nature. A person with a strong character is not likely to be influenced by the gaze because his own nature will protect him.

Another way to manipulate is through good example, as it is always said *"an example is worth a thousand words"*. Such as the following story that can be inspiring:

"In Japan, the story goes that a man went out to look for a rose and searched for a long time without being able to find it. The new flowers he found had beauty, but they did not match the rumors he had heard about their immeasurable beauty and the greatness of their perfume. In his long search he met the amaryllis that swayed on their flexible stems, showing their beautiful brown spots. He also enjoyed the peonies and their pleasant scent, with their flaming bush shape. He appreciated the acacias, with the stalactites that dominated the surroundings. The crimson carnations with their green calyxes, the lilies that wore their black color proudly and many more that came to captivate his senses. This man came to the conclusion that none of them was the rose he had heard about. He had given up hope when he saw a beautifully colored butterfly resting on a bush. A wonderful perfume seemed to come from it as it gently fluttered its wings. The man, with great surprise, approached it and said to it:

-Beautiful creature, who wears bright colors and exhales a sweet perfume, is it possible that you are the rose?

No," the butterfly replied, "I am not the rose, but I live very close to it, I enjoy its bows and branches in bloom, I sleep in the hollow of its small corollas and I feed on the sweet perfume emanating from its flowers. That is why I am so impregnated with its scent and have succeeded in deceiving you."

This serene and descriptive account is excellent for introducing a text or a dissertation and positively predisposing the listener or reader to what comes next.

Each person who hears such stories makes his own interpretation and his own positive associations. The thought that is generated in one surround center of the brain is projected to the other brains which may be of a weaker caliber so that they register it mechanically and then reproduce it.

A speaker should be able to influence his listeners in a positive way, achieving a transmutation of negative and selfish thoughts into altruistic ideas that seek the common good. In some cases, this influence will be temporary and in others it will be definitive. In the first case, the fear of change may be the reason why the influence is temporary or because the person understood that such change does not suit him/her.

Another way to manipulate is to plant an idea in people's minds. Depending on what the idea is, this technique can bring great benefits to mankind. Although it is often used for selfish purposes, such as advertisements, with the intention of directing people's attention in a certain direction. It is a powerful technique and works on the following pattern:

"Is ... (here mentioned the subject to be expounded) ... (a statement on said subject)?"

This statement is an attribute of the topic and can be either positive or negative, depending on what you hope to achieve from your listeners. The answer may be a yes or no answer. It can also be a rhetorical question that covertly expresses an opinion.

For example:

Are vibration platforms an option to maintain muscle tone for different age groups?

Can vibration platforms be dangerous for individuals who have a prosthesis or for those who have heart problems?

Are Doberman breed dogs the best guardians for a home?

These seemingly innocent-looking questions direct the listener's attention to the topic to be addressed and may cast doubt on the listener's beliefs. Intrigue is also introduced or intellectual curiosity is aroused. This technique has variations on its original pattern in order to create new patterns that act differently, but achieve the same effect. For example:

Have you noticed that...?

Did you notice ...?

Do you understand that...?

Do you consider that...?

Did you ever think that...?

The introductory sentences could then read as follows:

Have you ever thought that the image shown by others can play in your favor or against you depending on the social concepts you measure yourself by?

Have you ever noticed that if you don't have a well-written resume it becomes difficult to find a job?

Have you noticed how important it can be to know two languages when it comes to getting a well-paying job?

For example: if the theme is self-improvement in the work environment, a way to introduce the topic could be "Did you know that Bruce Lee, the great martial artist, used to say that you have to flow like water because it is soft, it adapts to spaces, but nothing bends its will to flow?" and thus introduce the topic of what the evolution of events means and what leads to self-improvement.

Another technique widely used when seeking to manipulate is to appeal to people's identity. Each person has his own identity that identifies him, that gives a kind of seal, so one way to persuade is to appeal to his identity and make him notice that he is valuable because of it.

According to businessman Dale Carnegie, who has studied efficient communication between people, says that people should be given a reputation that they will strive to achieve and maintain. There are several ways to make a person have a reputation, based on the following pattern:

"I can truly tell you that you are a person who... (identity)... because (the reason why you are being given this identity is stated)."

For example:

"I can tell you're a very smart person, because you're running a very difficult race."

"I can tell you that you are a person who seeks high standards because you have decided to grow in your work. "

This generates an identity pattern for the person and gives him or her membership in a certain group, thus utilizing the need for affiliation. A variant of this technique is to use a word scheme such as *"open-mindedness"*. If you ask a group of people if they are open-minded, 90% of them will answer yes. This is because by comparison they would be closed-minded and, by achieving the consensus of open-minded people, it is much easier for them to accept the idea presented to them in order to maintain the status of an open-minded person. A variant to this premise is to phrase the sentences as follows:

"How open-minded can your mind be enough to test the following alternatives? "

"How open is your mind to allow us to work together?"

"How open is your mind to implement this method to increase your monthly income? "

Another way to reference a person's identity, when there is not much knowledge about him/her, is to use the following pattern:

> *"I bet you're like me, even if it's just a little bit and ..."*

The first part of the sentence marks an agreement and that will facilitate agreement in the second part of the sentence. For example:

"I bet you're like me, if only a little bit, and you'd rather enjoy a job that will pay very good dividends in the near future."

"I bet you're like me, even if it's just a little bit and it bothers you to waste time in front of the TV."

"I bet you're like me, even if it's just a little bit and you have so many occupations that you juggle time to be able to meet all your obligations."

In addition, it is common for the listener to make some mental representations in his or her mind, in accordance with the speech he or she is listening to. This is a natural and normal process while listening to a new idea or also when remembering ideas we already have. Therefore, this fact also becomes a manipulation tool. For this reason, speakers use images because they are aware of this process and know that it will help them in their speech. For example: if the speaker says that he saw a beautiful bird flying over the mill and heading for the mountain, the audience will have that image in his head. If he then says, suddenly the fog erased all my images, the same thing will happen in the head of every listener.

There are other phrases that will make it a bit more complex to imagine, but this will help to sow confusion in the listener's mind. For example:

"Understanding the idea that follows is easy.

"Understanding the idea that follows is not difficult."

In both sentences you are saying the same thing but the mental images that originate from there can be very different in each person. When you start the dissertation with sentences like *"imagine that..." or "suppose that..."* you are giving the mind the possibility to free itself and live its own imagination in the direction you give it later.

If the audience is told about their favorite subjects the mental images will come out very easily. This is the process that occurs when we read a book. As you go through it, the images appear and you could almost say that you can see it like a movie in your mind. The television, the cinema and everything that is visual limits the possibility of freeing the imagination because the images are already there.

A skilled communicator knows the key to success and applies it. The liberation of the imagination together with the sensitive personalization of the message is the most effective cocktail to make the listener feel attracted to the message. This message, said in this way, managed to touch his most sensitive fibers and this fact predisposes him positively to accept what he is being told.

CHAPTER 6
POSITIVE REINFORCEMENT AND NEGATIVE REINFORCEMENT

"Stay away from the people who try to

dwarf your ambitions.

Little people always do that,

but really great people,

Makes you feel that you too can be great."

Mark Twain

Positive reinforcement: this type of reinforcement is a way of recognizing the other person's actions and compensating for them as a way of valuing them. Positive reinforcement is a reward for having performed a good action or a good job. This valorization increases the likelihood that good behaviors will be repeated.

It is totally normal for human beings to like to be recognized for their work, their services and their efforts. It means that you are not invisible to others and that what you did makes a difference between not doing any action and doing it, as well as being taken into account.

People who profess the Catholic religion think that they have to do good so that God will reward them in heaven. It is also often used as a crutch with children to get them to do good deeds. In addition, they are told that if you behave badly God will punish you.

For example:

"This month you will get an extra bonus for increasing productivity. "

"You earned a sweet treat for putting away your toys. "

"You don't have homework today because you finished the assignment on time in class. "

"This present is because you helped me study. "

In general, positive reinforcement is used to make the person understand that his or her actions brought benefit that is appreciated. While there are people who reward because they truly value what they do for them, it is also true that manipulators use positive reinforcement to manipulate their victims. The mind connects this reinforcement as a consequence of what they did, so they are very likely to perform either the same or similar actions again to gain the approval of others. How you felt when you were rewarded is also recorded in your mind.

Manipulators seek reinforcement to generate a behavior that benefits them, giving as a message *"if you do not criticize what I do, you will have a reward that is to your liking"*. For example: the boss who compensates his employee so that he does not say that he is diverting company funds to his personal account.

Even the reward can be such that a person will perform an action that he or she would not normally perform. This is where the person's moral values come into play. Manipulators will go to great lengths to achieve their goal by numbing the person's senses and value judgments. It is important to note that, if successful the first time, they will attempt to achieve other goals with the same person they were able to manipulate.

It is also very possible that the victim thinks that he/she is important in the victimizer's life and this gratitude strengthens the relationship between them, generating trust between them. Some manipulators approach a person saying "you're so smart" and then ask for a favor claiming that they can't do it because they have intellectual limitations. It is up to you to let them know that you noticed their manipulation and whether or not to do them the favor they request.

Among the positive reinforcements is the fact of persisting. Persisting is a fact of the positive type that invites one not to give up in the face of adversity and to stick to one's goal, which is why it is a starting point for manipulators.

Persistence is natural in human beings and is one of the most common ways in which human beings communicate. It must be taken into account that, within certain limits, it is harmless and even necessary, acting on the individual in a positive way.

Put another way: persistence is an interaction between people in which one person repeatedly makes a request, while the other repeatedly ignores it. The battle will end when one of the two people changes their will: either the requester stops requesting, or the other person ends up agreeing.

For example:

"I'm not leaving here until you change that mirror. "

"I'm not going to shut up until you quit smoking. "

"Start the diet as soon as possible because your complaints about not being able to do it are your big limitation and I'm going to be here to remind you. "

Parents often use persistence all the time with their children in order to get them to learn habits that benefit their health. Persistence used in this way has its positive aspects. But in the case of manipulators, there is a good chance that its application will not be beneficial to the victim. One way to know if the person who acts in a persistent manner has good or bad intentions is to ask the following questions:

Are you requesting something that only benefits her?

Is there any kind of threat within what you are manifesting?

Do you flatter me maliciously within your persistence?

Do you use guilt in your speech to try to convince me?

Do you express your speech accompanied by the expression "otherwise it will happen..."?

In general, persistence is considered to be the key to achieve work or professional and also economic success. It is also a way to strengthen character, willpower and also self-esteem. It can also develop a sense of commitment and vision for the future. Likewise, it stimulates the patience so necessary to fight for a goal without giving up.

For example:

Walt Disney was shunned in his early days for being considered untalented at cartooning. He used to say that success depended on not giving up.

The Wright brothers were criticized for the idea of wanting to build machines to fly. Had they not persisted they would not have achieved their first flight with their Kitty Hawk.

Enrico Caruso was rejected by all the singing teachers of his time because he was considered incapable of singing. He was self-taught and achieved undisputed fame, being able to break glass with his voice.

Bruce Lee was nearsighted, had a deviated spine and one leg shorter than the other. That didn't stop him from going far in the martial arts, becoming a Kung Fu master and inventing his own martial art, Jeet Kune Do.

Another form of persistence is the so-called *"love bombing"* which is widely used when you hope to conquer someone. The difference is that the person who exercises it does not expect only a love relationship, but hopes to manipulate his victim with different intentions. That someone you have just met initiates this bombardment is a reason to be suspicious, because rarely do people display such generosity only with altruistic intentions. If the victim allows the person to advance in this method, she is allowing her subjugation with the danger of losing her identity, her friendly environment and it is very likely that she will also lose control of her money. All this, surely, will also lead her to lose her mental health.

Love bombing is very effective, especially if the person has low self-esteem or is a bit isolated. That is why it is widely used by fraudsters who target elderly people who do not have a lot of attention from their relatives.

In this way, the victim's heart is immediately touched and his or her trust is gained. The person who applies it is pleasant, charismatic, well-mannered and naturally strikes up a good conversation with the victim. Everything happens so quickly that the victim does not even realize what is really going on. The predator using this technique showers the person with attention that he or she has never had before, and the person is so comforted that he or she becomes attached to the predator very easily.

Negative reinforcement or punishment: in the same way that positive reinforcement is applied for performing the expected action, there is also negative reinforcement in which an action considered negative is prevented from being carried out. Sometimes it is considered as a punishment, but some researchers prefer to differentiate negative reinforcement from punishment, considering the latter as a negative action that tries to exemplify the person who performs actions that should not be performed. This reinforcement is also used by manipulators to pressure victims to achieve their purposes. In general, it is psychological pressure that is exerted.

For example:

"If you don't wash the dishes tonight, tomorrow you'll find them full of ants. "

"Brush your teeth so you don't get cavities. "

"If you don't do your tax filing you're going to get a penalty. "

"Raise your productivity if you don't want to lose this job. "

"If you don't train every day don't expect to win the competition. "

"If you don't have the surgery your husband is sure to cheat on you. "

"If you bring good grades from school, you won't have to clean your room. "

These examples show that negative reinforcement is more frequent than is generally believed. These reinforcements strengthen the expected responses, whereas punishment ends up weakening them. Moreover, it is demotivating.

Why is it called negative if it is producing positive behavior? The point is that this positive behavior is produced by fear. For example: if someone stops smoking because he is afraid of cancer, he is seeking a positive action that is born from a fear. Negative reinforcement can also bring about problematic actions, because the person receiving it is undergoing a psychological action that can accumulate frustrations and anger. Many times the person complies because he/she wants to end the negative stimulus that is chasing him/her.

A great disadvantage of this reinforcement is that it generates a stressful environment in all aspects of life. If it is applied in the home environment it will lead to distrust among its members.

In the workplace it will encourage competition based on every man for himself, instead of stimulating companionship and teamwork. With this reinforcement, conflicts, mistrust and negative emotions will be promoted, although at first it may seem that a specific problem is being solved.

The pressures exerted by some nations with an important economic development on others that have not achieved the same, generates a negative reinforcement that will lead to submission due to fear of the consequences.

One form of negative reinforcement is the "silent treatment". This treatment is as if the manipulator is saying: if you do not do what I ask you to do, I withdraw my love. It is widely used in people who have a strong emotional dependency or after having practiced love bombing. Once this technique is applied, it leaves the person ready for this second technique to achieve the proposed objective.

This silent treatment, in the work environment, makes the person feel diminished, devalued and even non-existent. This affects their emotions to a greater or lesser extent depending on their particular characteristics. In this way, the person feels the threat of losing both the place he/she conquered, in the case of a job, and the love he/she conquered in the case of a partner.

The predator sows the seed of fear and doubt, using phrases such as "I love you, but you need to understand..." or "here you have a place that you earned by your merits, but this new person who entered...". These phrases are always devastating to the emotions and feelings of some people, whose nature is sensitive. In your mind you will begin to search your memory for which of all your actions made you angry and so begins the feeling of guilt. Guilt is a feeling that marks a reference between what should be and what is, or between what was done and what should have been done. Some people feel guilty all the time because they were raised that way. The manipulator sees guilt as a gateway into the psyche of his victim.

CHAPTER 7

MANIPULATION OF CIRCUMSTANCES

"With skillful manipulation of the press,

can make the victim look like a criminal

and the criminal, a victim."

Malcolm X

Manipulation of circumstances is also a technique for manipulating people. Although it is often used in combination with the others. Manipulating a circumstance means that, using real events, you give them a focus that is convenient by omitting details, taking phrases out of the real context, increasing or decreasing the importance of some attitudes and thus giving a personal touch to what really happened.

Language is rich in nuances and is ambiguous enough to narrate circumstances from different points of view, making several versions. A manipulative person who is skilled in oratory can turn an event on its head.

For example: a child predator will be able to convince his little victim that he is the only person who loves her. Then, as time goes by, he will convince the victim that she has to leave his side to live her life because it is in her best interest. The child predator is interested at a certain age; as the victim grows older, he ceases to be interested.

Another example is the case of lawyers defending a criminal. The facts are distorted to remove the responsibility of their defendant. This is done to try to win the case regardless of whether the offender is guilty or not.

One way to exercise this manipulation technique is to resort to excuses. This modality is frequent when one seeks to avoid responsibility for events. Excuses are used in all walks of life and at all ages. All human beings have invented excuses at some point in their lives and in general it has been to avoid the truth before other people.

Another way to manipulate the facts is to blame the victim because he or she is the one who triggered the events. The perpetrator convinces the victim that this is the case and most victims believe it.

For example: it is common for a battering man to tell his partner that he got angry because of her and that he had no choice but to hit her because he deserved it for her bad behavior.

This method works with victims who have been isolated from their environment and do not find where to get support to share and get another point of view. In addition, it is certain that there are feelings that bind the victim to the perpetrator and this leads to justification.

A variation of fact manipulation is to withhold information by telling the same facts but more strategically. Knowing how to respond to a given piece of information, the storyteller will manage to accommodate the truth so that the information benefits him or her because the details will be hidden. It is widely used by politicians because it allows them to manipulate the facts as they wish.

Another way to use this technique is to exaggerate certain parts of the story, making it sensationalist or minimizing certain actions for their own benefit. Used by advertising and marketing agencies, as well as by public relations and the media.

In order to achieve ratings, some media manipulate information by sensationalizing it, mainly in the headlines, which are the first thing that attracts the attention of readers. This method can be used to discredit people, societies and even nations. It was used in the Cold War and was called psychological warfare. Truths were told half-truths and from a very subjective point of view.

Another way to manipulate circumstances is intimidation. Intimidation is the way to bend the will of another person by touching his or her most sensitive points. It can be done directly or indirectly, depending on what is needed and, in general, it is initiated in a subtle way.

The direct bully is angry or furious and gives orders to others shouting, acting with a threatening attitude, difficult to contradict. He can exercise this manipulation in verbal form or raise it to a higher level and reach the point of physical violence. Indirect or covert intimidation appears to be gentler, but it is a slow and inexorable work. The manipulator is also a violent person, but disguises it by showing his gentle and charismatic side.

These people are really dangerous because they know how to hide their nature very well and the victims manage to realize it when the relationship is already advanced and it becomes difficult to get out of that place. Sometimes the victim is so emotionally and psychologically hurt that he/she is unable to realize that he/she is living a hell. Indirect bullies have many strategies and use them in a cold and calculating way. Their methods are highly effective and in most cases they achieve their goal.

Sometimes intimidation can be positive. For example: it is psychologically proven that if a person intends to steal in a supermarket in a disguised way, suddenly someone looks at him seriously and fixedly, he feels intimidated and recognized, abandoning his intention to steal. His bad intentions lead him to think that everyone else has them too, and in his mind begins the idea that he will become a victim if he goes ahead with his original idea.

In a boxing match, the boxers look at each other in an intimidating way and if one of them allows this intimidation to affect him, it is certain that he will lose the fight before the fight begins. By allowing himself to be intimidated, he will have less chance of winning than if he does not allow himself to be affected by the intimidation. In reality, this intimidation is simply pre-fight advertising for higher ratings.

At the time of the Beatles and the Rollings Stones, there was a lot of publicity about them being enemies and competing with each other. But it was just a publicity stunt, because in their personal lives they were friends and had no problems with each other. But in public life they made intimidating statements.

There are stories for children that work on intimidation to achieve certain behaviors in them. For example: the children's song that says: "Go to sleep child, go to sleep now, the bogeyman is coming and will eat you." It is a form of bullying that has become naturalized. In other children's stories, bullying becomes terrifying.

Intimidation, when it is covert, is almost certain to convince the victim. In contrast to direct intimidation, which is overtly manifested verbally or with physical violence, affecting the victim's psyche. In general, all victims find it difficult to get rid of their predator.

Whenever the manipulator wants to maintain control for an extended period of time, intimidation will have to be constantly fed. In addition to his phrases and body language, he uses drama that emphasizes what he is saying. In these cases, violence, anger and anger are his preferred tools because he manages to make a visual impact that can terrify the victim. The victim will try to pacify the moment so that it does not become an extreme situation. In reality, he does it because he is afraid of it and cannot find a way to free himself from this vicious circle.

The victim feels guilty and this guilt is a feeling that marks a reference between what should have been and what is. If the person has received strict training, he or she will feel guilt more easily. All these manipulated circumstances will serve for the person to form a mental idea of how the behavior to which he will have to adjust should be. Every time his behavior differs from what is mentally stipulated, the person will feel guilt. This guilt will be used to reach the deepest parts of the victim's psyche, disintegrating his personality and his will.

In general, guilt triggers feelings of shame and also of regret, which will need to be elaborated and transcended in a healthy way in order to return to being oneself. Each individual has a certain level of guilt that is related to the level of self-demand that he/she possesses. The higher the level of self-demand, the higher the level of guilt felt because it is almost certain that the individual seeks to get as close as possible to perfection. When he sees that his behavior moves away from the perfection he imagines in his mind, he begins to feel guilt.

This guilt is also associated with feelings of anguish, fear, sadness, anxiety and uncertainty. All of them may refer to situations that occurred in childhood because they are the most vulnerable points of all people.

A manipulator who knew how to get close enough to the victim, surely talked to her and knows her weaknesses, fears and will bring them out at the right time making the victim feel ashamed of her mistake or her actions.

For example:

- Guilt will be manipulated to end the person's self-esteem.
- Continually remind her of her mistakes so that the victim feels guilty because she is not as perfect as she would like to be.
- He accompanies guilt management with silent treatment, minimization of his skills and rejection.
- Make the victim feel that under no circumstances is he or she up to the task.
- Use social isolation, suggesting that people stay away from her because of her big mistakes and the ease with which she makes

mistakes.

In any aspect of life, the manipulator will find a way to make this person feel guilty, trying to make this level of guilt increase. If this person's critical thinking were functioning, it is possible that he or she would realize the work the manipulator is doing. But the opinions of this predator, unfortunately, carry so much weight within the psyche of the manipulated person that he or she does not, under any circumstances, question what he or she is saying or the intentions he or she has in saying it.

When the victim becomes aware of it, it is very important that he/she gets away from the person who was manipulating him/her for good. If it is a person that you see within your work environment, you will have to learn to be strong enough to not give importance to what he/she says. This is going to be very difficult to implement, but if it is not possible to walk away, then you have to deal with the situation in whatever way you can and with the utmost fortitude.

Another option is to tell the person up front that he has already worked out his own conflicts and that nothing he says is going to affect him. Therefore, they should not continue to waste their energy because their actions will no longer be positive.

At this point, you have to be careful that the manipulative person does not turn around and start saying "too bad you misunderstood my ideas" and then start moving into another technique that leads you to think that you are free to choose. It is important to keep in mind that a manipulative person will always be manipulative with his thousands of tricks and presenting himself as an innocent person with good intentions.

At this tipping point, then, nothing that comes from this person will be listened to no matter how reasonable it may seem. For it is here that you can use the premise "you are free to choose".

Then the person does not feel the pressure, but rather their options seem to be liberated by being able to choose. There are studies that show that this option facilitates the acceptance of what is being proposed.

For example:

"(Asking for something) but you are free not to accept."

"(Asking for something) although of course you are under no obligation to do so."

"(Asking for something) but logically it's up to your choice."

Phrased in this way, the person believes he has the option to choose, but this feeling of inner freedom will lead him to accept what is proposed to him.

CHAPTER 8
HOW TO SOW DOUBT

"Whenever you teach,

teaches at the same time

to doubt what you teach."

José Ortega y Gasset

Another way in which you can also master manipulation is to learn to control a conversation. Regardless of whether the interlocutors are passive or active, whether there are *"know-it-alls"* who hope to hog the spotlight or people with ingrained beliefs who are unwilling to change their ideas, learning to control a conversation is one of the greatest skills of a manipulator.

The technique used in these cases is called *"sowing doubt"*, in which a panorama of doubt or uncertainty about an issue is given, so that it leads to rethinking the basis on which it is believed.

The conversation moves from a principle of certainty, which can be raised by any interlocutor, to a perspective of doubt or uncertainty in a direct questioning that leads the person to self-question his or her own beliefs. When in the group that is conversing, there is a person who is difficult to convince, this technique can be combined with the one in which the person is told *"you are free to choose"* which, in this case, is replaced by *"you are free to believe whatever you want"*.

When seeking to challenge a firm mindset, it is necessary to go to its foundations. The objective will be, in this case, for the person to admit that his or her beliefs are based on insufficient evidence.

One way to do this is to raise within the conversation:

"What do you know about...?"

Thus, uncertainty is raised on the basis of belief.

For example:

"What do you know about the benefits we are discussing in this conversation? "

"What do you know about the way things work on this site? "

"What do you know about the economic and political situation that led to trigger the events that are being raised today?"

"What do you know about the fundamentals that initiate these concepts I am expounding here today?"

"What do you know about this business and in what way are the actions implemented? "

In this way, all the people present will start to reflect on what is being said. Even if their intention is not to reflect, the seed of doubt has been sown and at some point it will emerge and take effect, even if it is not at the moment of the conversation. When this happens, the person becomes a little more receptive to new concepts.

It is necessary that at all times the exchange of words takes place in an atmosphere of calm and peaceful interaction. Because if the conversation unleashes passions, it is likely that the person you are trying to convince will become defensive and instead of taking a receptive attitude, closing the possibility of dialogue.

These phrases must be used free of emotions, with confidence, security and coherence, without forgetting that everything must be raised in a climate of respect for differences.

A complementary technique to sowing doubt is learning to change the direction of the conversation. Directing the topic where the speaker wants it to go is a skill that is very useful when you have an audience with a short attention span.

In this way, you change the direction of the thoughts of the people with whom you are conversing. This technique can also be used to move the conversation from one topic to the next. In other words, the conversation has taken a direction that does not suit the manipulator and the manipulator subtly applies the technique and takes the conversation where he is interested.

These techniques have a very broad application as they can be used in everyday life as well as in the workplace, not to mention in those social opportunities where it is appropriate to shift the attention of the conversation from one instance to the other. Although it is a manipulation technique, it can also be used for the benefit of a group. Suppose a conversation is getting difficult, then with this technique, you will be diverting the conversation to a topic that is uplifting or more positive for the people who are listening.

The pattern usually used for this technique is:

"The issue is not... (here you introduce the other person's point of view) but... (and here you introduce your own point of view)" then you express a question that will act as a link to get to the focus of the issue you are looking for.

For example:

"The issue is not the insecurity that can be seen in the suburbs of the city, but the few possibilities to go for a leisurely walk", "how are you exercising your muscles so that they don't lose their tonicity? "

"The issue is not high oil prices in the Middle East, but bombings in places where the victims are innocent people, even if it is in far away places on the planet", "what are the measures that governments should take preventively to make peace a real reality? "

In this subtle and organized way, it is possible to change the subject without analyzing too much how it was changed. Another way to apply this technique is as follows:

Suppose we need to convince a group of business people to conduct a seminar that includes an addendum on in-company communication training. But this group is too preoccupied with their financial issues that they are unable to resolve. Then the technique could be applied as follows:

"The problem does not lie in the economic benefits that are obtained individually in each of their companies, but rather it can be seen that there is a lack of good communication with their workers, who do not manage to satisfy the problem due to the lack of adequate advice. What is missing in their work teams to increase and optimize their performance?"

This small dissertation will shift the focus to the communication problems that may exist between the work teams and the hierarchical teams, who fail to get their messages down. Thus, the conversation will be focused on the lack of communication and how to solve them. The need for the seminar will be introduced.

Employers may begin to question the price of the seminar and the time it will take to conduct it. Then you can say, "The issue is not how much the seminar costs, but how much this return has cost each of you, which is far below what you can expect. If you were able to visualize the return on investment that this seminar has, would you be willing to invest the cost and time that the seminar needs?"

In conclusion, every time the conversation wanted to take a path that is not convenient, it is always possible to apply the above pattern to redirect the attention to what you want to achieve.

Another technique that can be used in a conversation to achieve the stated objective is the DTR method or *"Disrupt then reframe"*, from which the acronym DTR was taken.

This technique is considered a mental trick rather than a manipulation technique. What cannot be denied is its effectiveness. The research on which this trick was based is attributed to Davis and Knowles, who, in 1999, made clear its effectiveness by making door-to-door sales of greeting cards. In order to collaborate with a local charity, the sales were carried out under two different strategies:

The first, these sales were taken as a reference and the person in the traditional way said they cost $2.50 for 5 cards, achieving a sale in 40% of the homes visited.

The second: these sales were presented as 250 cents for 5 cards, adding the phrase *"it's a real bargain", in this* way they managed to sell in 80% of the homes visited.

Just by changing the way of presenting the sale, twice as many sales were achieved at the same price. What is it that makes the result so different? What happens in the minds of the people who receive the information? The DTR works because it interrupts the usual thought process because, normally you would hear dollars and not cents, when you hear the word cents, you are left thinking why use this word when you could say dollars? and after this interruption of normal thinking, comes the phrase *"a real bargain"*. Then the person falls into the fact that he is being sold something cheap.

It is important to mention that this whole situation only takes place in a few seconds where the person is confused by the interruption of thought he/she had.

If the person knows how to get out of this confusion quickly and returns to his critical thinking, he will realize that it is a deception and it is very likely that he will not fall for it. The faster the salesperson is, the lower the chances that the person will react and the technique will be a success. This trick can be combined with the scarcity technique, saying that there are only a few left. This will make the decision a little quicker.

This technique was then tested in 14 subsequent investigations involving hundreds of participants. These studies were conducted by Carpenter & Boster in 2009. The results obtained were surprising for the effectiveness of this simple technique. In these studies it was seen that, through the application of the technique, people are able to change their attitude, complete surveys and, logically, increase the number of sales.

This DTR technique has even been effective in those situations in which a person normally distrusts the salesperson's trickery. In short, it is a very convenient strategy when a certain result is expected to be achieved. Its application will depend on the moral limits of the person who is going to apply it.

If you do not want to be a victim of this situation, it is important to maintain critical thinking at all times, as well as not to be rushed or overwhelmed with phrases.

Another way of controlling the conversation and directing it at will is the use of compound suggestions. In this technique, all suggestions that are made on the topic being discussed are accepted and then steered in the direction that is needed.

The technique that can be used to get someone to accept the suggestion that is being made to them is called "using compound suggestions". It is a technique that is based on the objective of maintaining a self-image that is consistent for others, followed by a suggestion that is the one you are trying to incorporate in the other person. The way to put it into practice is simple, you have to say something that has a good chance of being shared and approved by the other person, i.e. a truth that is tacitly accepted. Next, you put the suggestion that you hope will be accepted. Generally speaking, the scheme would be:

"Self-image, opinion or accepted fact...plus suggestion that you want to get the other person to accept."

For example:

"Communication within the company is fundamental to achieve excellent performance, without double messages. "

"Your company is in need of communication across all its sectors to improve so I suggest this seminar. "

"You come home from work and rest on your couch as usual. It would be gratifying to fall into a little restful sleep. "

For total success in all areas of life, it is essential to have the ability to persuade the people you work with. To achieve this, it is important to know the proper methods as contained in this book.

A good appearance and friendliness are the key to open the doors of many work environments. A good resume is the guarantee that completes this combo. With this course you will learn how to do it impeccably.

To achieve the weight I need, it is necessary for me to go on a diet. This book is able to analyze your calories from simple exercises ideal for weight loss.

In addition, there is the sentimental issue. If all these evocations include scenarios with feelings, the effect will be much more effective.

A complementary technique is to state *"I agree with what you say and I would add that..."*

With this pattern a framework of agreements is achieved from which the particular thought that the persuader wants to use is incorporated. This technique has a positive effect because by saying "I agree" it lowers the guard of the person who was on the defensive, and it narrows down what you want the person to consider. Even if at first there is total disagreement, this technique brings the positions closer together.

In this way, agreements can be reached and conditions that cannot be refused can be restated. This technique depends in part on the sympathy and *rapport* of the speaker or the persuader or manipulator who intends to use the technique.

The principle on which this technique is based is that people like to have their opinions and ideas taken into account. By telling them I agree, they will be satisfied, even if the idea that is then put forward goes in the complete opposite direction.

The pattern usually used is:

"I agree and, furthermore, I would add that...."

For example:

"I agree that the seminar is expensive and would add that, beyond its price, it is going to earn me a good percentage by increasing performance. "

"I agree that the work schedules are exaggerated and would add that this is a temporary effort that is going to regularize shortly. "

It is a versatile technique that adapts very easily to what you are trying to expose. Used in the middle of a dissertation, it can create a bit of confusion that will make listeners pay a little more attention.

CHAPTER 9
HOW TO REALIZE IF WE ARE BEING MANIPULATED

"Stop letting people

who does so little for you,

control so much of your mind,

your feelings and emotions."

Will Smith

It is frequent that the person who manipulates others tends to be charismatic and it is difficult to think that his actions are malicious because in appearance he appears to be sincere and honest. His work is elaborate, subtle, professional, well planned and his actions are not appreciated until some time has passed and the facts have been analyzed.

It is common that the manipulator, by filling emotional voids, causes the rational aspects of the manipulated person to close down and the manipulated person does not have a good perspective of reality. It is also possible that the manipulator treats his victim as if he were his puppet.

For all these reasons it is essential to be attentive and learn to see the signs that distinguish a manipulator. It is not necessary to be able to distinguish which technique is used, it is enough to realize that this person is trying to manipulate us.

In the case of wanting to analyze a couple's relationship, in order to know if they are exercising manipulation, the following points can be looked at:

When you are happy to have found love, but soon after the joy transforms into a fear of losing what you have achieved. Your feelings of happiness turn into sadness, anguish and sometimes despair.

Your emotions have no middle ground, it goes from a state of fullness to a state of emptiness without mediating a conflict situation.

The relationship also moves from fullness to emptiness for no reason.

The relationship is perpetuated over time, even if you don't feel comfortable when you are together.

You feel responsible for all events that occur.

You begin to feel guilty about the other person's unhappiness.

The relationship became complex and you have no idea how they got to that point.

You are obsessed by the relationship to such an extent that you are talking about it all the time.

You are on the defensive all the time, in a continuous state of alertness.

You feel jealousy, insecurities, anyone who approaches your partner becomes a mortal enemy.

You are watching every single thing your partner does all the time.

You try not to talk to your partner about what bothers you.

You usually put on a mask of happiness so that your true feelings do not show.

A great sense of guilt will develop and you will try to fix the damage you supposedly caused.

You sabotage the relationship without noticing it, then you realize it and wonder why you do it.

Perhaps not all of the symptoms are present or you get to have all of the feelings described. But if some are present, it is a reason to start thinking that you are suffering from your partner's manipulation.

If you have doubts and want to get a full understanding of the situation, it is recommended to consult a professional for a more detailed evaluation.

The first feeling you will have is confusion because the manipulator will try to make you doubt yourself. It will also make the manipulated person feel that their intuition is failing, that they doubt every decision, that they do not understand both verbal and non-verbal messages.

Thus will begin the dichotomy between understanding what is being done wrong and how one should act. The person feels loneliness, isolation from the rest of the world, because the manipulator will try to keep him away from all social relationships. Thus a relationship of obedience and submission will begin.

If a person is trying to manipulate you, they will do everything they can to install insecurity at the forefront of your emotions and thoughts. If you are doubtful of your self-esteem, he will do everything he can to lower it and make it hang by a thread. In addition, he will try to keep you away from your social environment because in this way the actions are facilitated for this person.

Being able to realize when they are trying to manipulate you, can be a skill that will collaborate with your own survival in today's society. In general, society is very competitive and in all aspects of life, especially in the workplace, many apply the *"every man for himself"* as if this crutch would keep them safe from many things. They defend their interests, impose their ideas and most of the time do not pay attention to who they are hurting. They may seek to make alliances by approaching you in a natural way and using manipulation to convince you.

A very common trait of manipulators is lying. These lies are either by commission or by omission. By commission is the classic type of lie, where something is said that is not true. It is a deliberate action that aims to deceive or mislead in order to obtain a certain advantage by this action. Also this type of lie is used to get out of a tight spot or because the person is afraid of the truth or because explaining it would take time and effort. Sometimes, the person lying may not have bad intentions, but may be ill.

Lying by omission is also known as "excluding details". That is, in this case a part of the truth is told and certain details are purposely omitted. They are elaborate and sophisticated lies because the person can get away with it if discovered, even if it is a legal situation, he/she can get away with it, claiming that the other person who asked was not specific enough about the details he/she had to give him/her.

The best example of this type of lie is when a salesperson gives specifications about a product that are very beneficial attributes, hiding the negative aspects of its use.

Another example in this regard: when someone makes two comments about another person: one in favor and one against. A third individual tells the person in question, in a manipulative way, the comment made against, because it will serve to take advantage of him.

When you fail to correct misconceptions that another person may have when you hear him or her say them, it is also a lie of omission.

These misconceptions can also be corrected at convenience by a manipulative person and he would also be lying by omission. For example: suppose there is a policeman outside a bank, the person who sees him thinks he is a custodian of the bank, but in reality he may be a policeman working elsewhere who went to the bank for a personal transaction.

An aspect that is also widely used by people who want to manipulate, is denial. Denial is indicating that the person does not accept reality for some reason. Manipulators use this weakness, feigning innocence when they know perfectly well what they are doing. It is a very strong control point, because denial has to do with some trauma and becomes a subtle but forceful mental abuse.

On the other hand, when directly confronting the manipulator, he/she will use denial in such a way that he/she will switch to the role of victim, turning all events upside down.

Denial is also used as a defense mechanism, as well as a manipulation tactic. On the other hand, it helps to avoid responsibility. In almost all cases, the other person will be psychologically damaged by using these processes.

In the same way that the predator is strengthened by the denial of his victim, he also knows how to give for a definite effect, the rationalization of the circumstances. It is necessary to understand that the person who manipulates is very skilled with language. Therefore, giving a meaningful rational context is simple. This is also a way to create excuses as reasonable versions of what you need the other person to believe.

Even if everything condemns the predator, there is a good chance that he will come out of the situation well because his level of rationalization is very good.

It is necessary to understand that, if someone expresses a concept in your presence and you do not tell him that you do not agree, the other person will understand that you agree with his thought and there will be a tacit agreement because your silence was taken as assent. And, logically, you will use it later. Therefore, if you do not agree with someone, it is essential that you tell them so as to leave no room for ambiguity.

If the manipulator does not resort to rationalization, he may resort to minimization. This psychological action is capable of triggering unexpected consequences. This is so because it directly affects the emotions and, for people who have low self-esteem, minimizing any issue that has to do with it will hurt their psychological aspects.

Parents have a habit of minimizing their children's anger because to the adult mind it seems exaggerated, although to the child it occupies a large place in his or her life. A manipulator may use both rationalization and minimization together, alternately, or adapt to present circumstances.

For example: when faced with a situation that the manipulator cannot rationalize, he/she will try to minimize it in order to put it in a context of exaggeration on the part of the victim.

Sometimes when you have achievements in life, there is always a person who will try to minimize it, either because it suits him or her or because of envy.

It often occurs in work environments, where the contributions made by one person to the success of a project are minimized by saying that it was teamwork. In a couple's relationship, the batterer may minimize the woman's crying because of the blows she received. The person on the receiving end of the minimization may feel psychologically self-conscious and frustrated, as well as belittled or left out.

On the other hand, there are manipulators who have the ability to understand all feelings at a very deep level, so they can become the victim's best confidants.

In this way, the predator can act like a chameleon and transform in an instant. In this case, it will act as a true mirror where the victim will be reflected in terms of emotions, feelings, tastes, preferences, current and past common situations achieving a level of coincidence in all aspects of life. These predators are also called personality readers and follow this technique in 3 levels that will ultimately elaborate the reflection. The first level, collects information from third parties hired for this purpose, making an exhaustive data collection. This information is expanded in their social networks, where many people have the habit of telling their lives. In the second level, the first encounters begin, which will be seen as casual, although they were coldly calculated. There the predator will make his confessions that will be similar to the events experienced by the victim, then the victim will be reflected and amazed for this reason. It will be unbelievable to her how much they resemble each other.

At the third level, the investigation and interactions deepen, reaching a level of trust as if they have known each other all their lives, and maybe it was only 15 days ago that they saw each other for the first time. These people act as if they are your soul mate and the person believes it. This is how this mirroring technique works, thanks to people's emotional needs and credulity.

CHAPTER 10
WHO ARE CAPABLE TO MANIPULATE US

"Every manipulator applies himself thoroughly.

to destabilize their victim in order to

to get her out of her mind in order to be able to

accuse her of being upset or unstable.

This helps him to manipulate it easily

from guilt."

Professor Iñaki Piñuel

Manipulators, as we have already said, are usually wolves in sheep's clothing. They use emotional blackmail by putting others at their disposal. They are great orators, they handle facts as they please and use cognitive distortion together with exploitation. They know how to create an imbalance to tip the balance in their favor and the manipulated person eventually goes on to live a life that is not what they imagined.

Manipulation can be present in different areas of life, as we will see below.

The retail sector: this is the most frequent use of manipulation and most people already know that there are many possibilities of being manipulated in favor of the purchase of the products. In general, people expect it and are surprised when they find an honest trader.

When a salesperson only guides the purchase, he is not looking for his own benefit but for the buyer to get the item that is convenient for him. Even if he makes the sale, he does so without manipulation, but rather gives the customer his best advice.

On the other hand, if the seller is persuading the buyer to take the more expensive item, he is manipulating the buyer and will probably charge a commission for the sale. They can be classified into 4 types of sellers according to the way they manipulate:

- **Power sellers:** are those who promise great benefits in exchange for their votes. They act by persuading and consider people as mere prospects to be convinced.
- **Money sellers:** they seduce with the intention of getting people to spend their money regardless of whether or not they need the product. They are only interested in getting their commission for the sales made.
- **Prestige sellers: they** seek public recognition within the environment in which they operate. They want admiration for their show or their lectures.
- **Sellers of ideas and attitudes:** they demonstrate that their values and philosophy are worth taking into account and adopting as their own. They are natural leaders, positive in some cases and negative without their followers noticing.

For example: if a person is only interested in the clothes he/she wears, it is almost certain that he/she will not be interested in reading a good book. Therefore, no matter how well the book is presented and whether it is of high quality, there is a good chance that this person will not buy it. But if he is offered the complete Oscar de la Renta collection, he will certainly buy it even if he has to go into debt to do so.

In general, there is an audience for every item, not forgetting that the big sellers and the big advertisements are designed to create the need for consumption of that product.

Marketers know perfectly well that it is difficult to change mindsets and tastes on an individual basis. That is why they create consumerist cultures that mark social groups to which people want to belong.

A few years ago, advertisements were talking in favor of smoking or drinking alcohol as the best way to achieve good social relations. It is also socially marked that a person is successful if they have a well-paying job, a well-built family, a house, a car or two, go on vacation every year and have a pedigree dog at the front door. If any requirement is not met, the person is likely to feel that he or she is stagnating in life.

Another example of manipulation is advertising that glorifies youth and, for this reason, many people who are past their prime want to regain it at all costs, through surgery or other methods. It is a culture in which aging seems shameful.

Salespeople will show an attractive image according to the beauty codes of the moment, trying to give prestige to the products. If they want to sell a car, they put it on the road through marvelous landscapes saying *"live without limits... Surrender to all kinds of sensations"*, without talking directly about the product. Unconsciously, the product is elevated to a certain prestige.

The manipulative salesman bases his effectiveness on the art of provoking reactions that are of the automatic type. That is why his speech will always have an accelerated pace to prevent the person from reflecting. If a certain soap is associated with the image of a beautiful young woman taking a happy shower, when going to buy soap, the unconscious will lead to that soap because the senses and emotions are hooked on that image. Then the person believes he is making a free choice, but in reality he is responding automatically to the stimulus he received. This manipulation is subtle and difficult to notice.

Ideologies: when they seek to manipulate ideologies on lifestyles, they use cunning to overcome popular opinion. They turn concepts upside down, they mark perspectives of planes on reality, they find a way to enunciate the ideas they seek to impose. It is important to understand that in all this there is a great emotional charge that will facilitate the acceptance of the ideology. These ideologies can become so strong that they come to divide nations, peoples and even some families.

But in recent years we have been hit by a pandemic that should make us reflect because it did not recognize borders, ideologies or social classes, it was overwhelming for all human beings who so meticulously insisted on creating differences and manipulating them. These differences were demolished with the stroke of a pen, revealing that the only thing that matters is the true essence of the human being.

Entrepreneurs: The position of entrepreneur is a position of power that fulfills its function within social development. It is a position that requires a certain talent, an entrepreneurial spirit and a great determination to face risks.

For the vast majority of entrepreneurs, employees are their "human material" that will allow them to achieve their business achievements, they are part of their machinery and their interest is that all their machinery works and functions correctly.

Employers who are sensitive to the dignity of their employees are concerned that each job has a real meaning for those who have to perform it and are aware of the importance that this work has in the final project. In certain cases, this ethics for workers has also been used as a form of manipulation, under the slogan "ethics is also profitable for the company".

Linking personal interests to the work project increases productivity, in the belief that the human quality of the workers is promoted.

Intellectuals: they have their own particular way of doing this, in particular, they distort events and beliefs, looking for scientific evidence and the vision that science can give of them. Their frequent crutch is that what is real can be proven through science and that everything that cannot be explained in this way, such as the fact that there is a God, corresponds to the irrational aspects of the individual and that they are superfluous beliefs to which they cling to give meaning to their lives.

Science does not have a humble position and does not recognize its limitations. This fact can be proven in all ages of mankind and if there had not been people who doubted what science said, today we would still think that the earth is flat and the center of the Universe.

It is time to admit that each discipline has its own limited aspects and that from all of them we can learn and enrich the knowledge of human beings. To take advantage of the prestige acquired by science and use it as a monopoly of truth is to limit other research options that are also real and viable. This scientific framework seems to invalidate everything that is outside it, even some research that tries to be incorporated into this framework.

A historical example of this is the discoveries of Nikola Testa, an incredible scientist who knew that his knowledge was not for his time but for future generations. He was never awarded a Nobel Prize, even though other scientists received it for their discoveries. The fact is that Nikola Testa claimed to receive information from the planet Mars and this fact disqualified him for the great prize, even though today many of his discoveries are being studied.

Education: in times where tyrants rule, the level of education of the population is often low. This is because people with little education are easy to convince because their critical judgment is underdeveloped. On the other hand, governments that call themselves democratic and hope to get the votes they need, make curricula in such a way that the ability to think, to draw conclusions, to discern and to put intellectual curiosity into practice is not stimulated. These are the attributes that human beings use to make an objective evaluation of the reality in which they live.

A person who has received the necessary education to develop critical judgment is not easily overwhelmed and will not be easily manipulated by an intellectual manipulator.

They usually proclaim their interest in culture, but this culture has a very directed interpretation, thus dominating thought. This culture generally puts science in the foreground to the detriment of the humanistic sciences and devaluing man's possibility for artistic creation.

This educational manipulation is often combined with ideological manipulation. Antonio Gramsci was able to elaborate a great tactic to achieve political power through cultural domination. This domination will be attempted through a process in which the ideas and feelings of the so-called intellectuals, are assumed by the majority and become a source of energy that marks a new morality from a different conception of the world. This conception is very likely to be quite distorted.

A well-understood education for people who belong to the people and that helps them to develop critical thinking, is fundamental for them to have a better chance to defend themselves from predators.

CONCLUSION

"All is lost when the bad guys

serve as an example and

the good ones of mockery."

Democrates

As you can see, becoming a victim of a manipulator has very serious consequences, so it is very important to keep the following in mind:

- A manipulator uses his ability to achieve his goals, impoverishing the victim's life and making him vulnerable.

- Persuasive action becomes so all-encompassing that it prevents rational thinking.

- The manipulated person often loses his or her identity, dignity and even personal values.

- The victim is torn between reality and the fiction that her predator created to convince the victim.

- The victim is alone, without the support of her family, self-doubting and distressed, in a state of confusion that leaves her disoriented and not knowing what to do.

- The persuader reduces the individual to his minimum expression so that he is totally under his control.

- The manipulator knows how to use language and his words always seem true, honest, generous, but we must not lose sight of the fact that he exercises demagogy and knows how to convince.

There will come a time when the victim will have his values disrupted, he will give himself up to instinctive processes believing that this is the way to feel full. He will have forgotten that fulfillment is achieved through values. These values, the higher they are, the richer they will be in nuances that lead the person to free himself from the fallacies with which a manipulator would try to envelop the person.

In this way, by disrupting values and without proper education, we return to primitive stages where only immediate satisfaction is sought. If to this is added the little projection of future for the youngest, the breaking point is accentuated in which delinquency increases, as well as fanaticism and society passes to a position of decadence, of a circle from which it seems that it is impossible to get out.

Humans, victims of manipulation, will have to reconnect with their family because their predator surely separated them with convincing arguments.

Individuals, victims of a manipulator, will certainly need the support of their family and professional treatment to put values back in place and to learn to view reality objectively.

This person will need to be taught how they were deceived and how they misrepresented their thoughts, emotions and feelings.

On the other hand, it is also necessary that you learn the process that leads to the comprehension and deep understanding of what happened, making your thinking more rational and less instinctive. Being aware of your weaknesses as well as your strengths will give you a different vision and prepare you to avoid falling into the hands of future predators.

In this way, he will be able to recover his ideals and get his life purpose back on track, returning to his true identity.

If you achieve mind control, you are aware of how you think and how you will react and it becomes difficult for someone to manipulate you. In addition, you will be able to detect these types of predators and you will also be able to prevent others in your environment from falling into manipulation.

It is always important to consider that a manipulative person is unscrupulous and upon detecting the weak points of his future victim, he will show no mercy and will use him whenever he can. Although the manipulator looks like a strong person, deep down he has low self-esteem and considers his life a disaster, believing that by destroying other people's lives he will make his own better.

They show great selfishness and their social skills allow them to cover up all their problems, being a friendly person, easily accepted in groups because they always know what they have to say to make themselves look good.

They are sometimes characterized by a low frustration tolerance. When situations are not within their expectations, they feel frustration and attack their future victim with sarcasm, sometimes even physical violence.

The manipulator has no limits in his requests, he is always asking for more and playing with the limits of his victim. In this way he satisfies his own ego as well as enjoying his victory because he achieves what he is looking for.

As we have already seen, there are many ways to manipulate others, some strategies are aggressive, others are subtle, others are active and others are passive. Manipulation in its most authentic expression is that which is carried out without the victim being aware of it. Without her noticing how the predator motivates her to behave in this or that way.

This is how they open the way to emotional blackmail and victimhood. In general, they assume the role of victims in front of their victims, with the intention of making them feel guilty. Some of these blackmails are direct with phrases such as "because of you I feel this way". Others are not so direct and blame third parties using a mechanism that narrates a message so that the current victim, in some way, feels identified and ends up saying "I also did something similar". This modality is much more effective than direct confrontation. Others will always be responsible for their future unhappiness.

Pressure accompanies this guilt mode, for example, when the victim is told *"if you don't help me with this job, I won't finish it on time and I might get fired"*.

Another way in which they attack their victims is by highlighting how much they sacrifice for others. They keep a sort of diary of everything they were able to do for your benefit. It has an exact count of every single thing they did.

If this method does not work, they use the action of ignoring. Pretending that the other person does not exist is a very cruel form of psychological mistreatment, even though it is passive, slow and subtle. Human beings show great sensitivity both to rejection and to being ignored: a look that is avoided or an expected word that is not said can have a profound effect on the victim.

The most common response of the victim in these cases is to withdraw into herself and avoid social contact. She has the exchange with others strictly indispensable, while the predator alternates between ignoring her and telling her that she is indispensable at work.

On the other hand, the predator includes victimhood by exploiting the idea of how much he has done for you. Don't forget that all this is designed to make you feel guilty. Also, in some cases, he will be able to use violence, bullying and destructive criticism. This destructive type of criticism can hurt the victim in many ways, especially if it occurs in the workplace.

Another way for the predator to retain the victim is to become dependent on her. He assumes a character that does not know how to manage on his own, that he is weak and needs a lot of help. In this way, he develops in the victim the feeling of being responsible for this being who came close enough to be a parasite.

Another way the manipulator can act is by playing the interpreter of everything that happens to you. These characters are Machiavellian and also aggressive. At first they will agree with what you say and your ideas, but they will be able to take your words and use them against you. In addition, they are able to find secret messages in the words you used. At this point it is essential to understand that language is ambiguous and you can always achieve different interpretations of what you say, especially if you are a skilled manipulator with words.

It can also incorporate sarcasm, which is always highly aggressive, sometimes indirectly. Veiled criticisms and humiliations degrade the victim and put the predator in a rank of superiority, giving a tacit contract of obedience of the victim to his manipulator.

There are also those who boast of their perfection and that anyone compared to them is ignorant and full of defects. Whenever they can, they point out their defects to others, generating insecurities and lack of faith in their possibilities. This is how they feed their ego.

If you think you are a victim of any of these characters, ask yourself the following questions:

- Do I feel guilty or inferior?

- Do I put myself aside and prioritize others in all types of relationships?
- Do I feel respected or abandoned?
- Do I feel that my needs are taken into account?
- Is what others are asking of me within the bounds of normal?
- Do I feel good about myself?

Analyzing how you feel is the starting point to begin to see if someone is manipulating you.

It is essential to be aware that all these feelings lead to the violation of your most basic rights. We all have the right to be treated with respect, to establish priorities as you understand them, you have the right to say that you do not feel guilty and you have the right to protect yourself against this type of mental, emotional and physical threats. Do not believe that you will be able to change the mentality of a manipulative person, they may make you believe that you can and use it to manipulate you. Manipulators do not change and it is best to stay away from them.

When true communication is achieved, when there are altruistic principles in the people who guide nations or human groups, the true flourishing of human beings is achieved. Knowing the fact that one can influence the thinking of other individuals, it is in the decision of each one to use it to achieve the common good and for personal relationships to be healthy and fruitful, free from manipulation.

Thank you for choosing my book to discover the power of dark psychology.

I hope you have learned during this trip!

If you like what you have read, I would like to have your opinion and positive feedback on the page where you bought it, because this way you help me reach more people and have a positive impact on their lives.

See you in the next book!

Greetings,

Robert Dawn

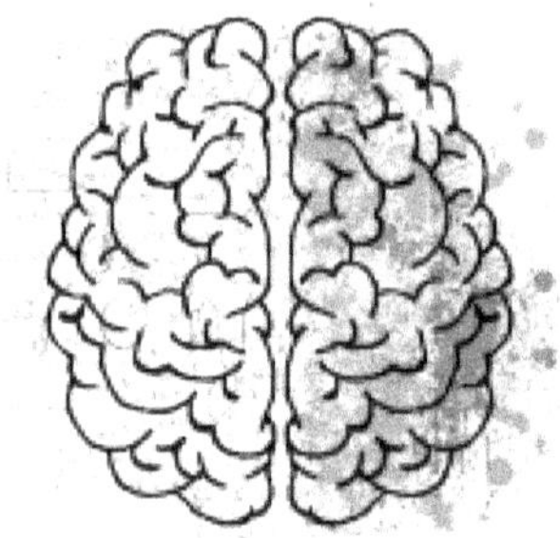

www.ingramcontent.com/pod-product-compliance
Lightning Source LLC
LaVergne TN
LVHW022023200926
848481LV00007B/2507
9798349660122